KNOW HOW KNOW WHY

THE AMERICAN CIVIL WAR

Written by Maria Smith

Illustrations by Mike Bell

TOP THAT! Kids™

Top That! Publishing Inc.
25031 W. Avenue Stanford, Suite #60, Valencia, CA 91355
www.topthatpublishing.com

THE PRE-WAR YEARS

In the years leading up to the American civil war, arguments about the power of the national government and the rights of individual states intensified. Leaders argued about the freedom of states to decide their own laws, and shouting turned into guerilla warfare over the legality of slave ownership in the Southern states.

Why did slave rights cause arguments ❓

The North and South had different economic needs and lifestyles. The Northern part of the United States was mainly industrial and wasn't suitable in either land or weather quality for an agricultural economy. On the other hand, the South was primarily agricultural, and crops such as cotton and tobacco were the major cash crops of the Southern economy. These needed heavy labor to maintain them, and slaves were used to do much of this hard work.

Who was arguing ❓

Charles Sumner.

Antislavery advocates and abolitionists were arguing with the Southern proslavery activists. Abolitionists were people who wanted slavery totally abolished. Charles Sumner, a distinguished senator from Massachusetts, was an antislavery advocate, and was beaten with a cane by Southerner Preston Brooks in 1856. The North thought this was a cruel action; however, the South hailed it with praise. John Calhoun, a spokesman from South Carolina, stood up for the agricultural way of life and slavery interests.

FACT BYTES

The most notable jayhawker of all was probably Charles R. "Doc" Jennison who briefly practiced medicine in Wisconsin before going to Kansas where he found horse stealing more profitable than medicine.

Why did some want a separate Southern nation

Southerners wanted a separate nation to justify the presence of slavery. Popular sovereignty referred to the political belief that the people of a territory or state, instead of the Federal government, had the right to decide whether slavery would be legal within their land. Many Southerners adopted this belief.

Who were the jayhawkers

"Jayhawkers" were anti-slavery pro-Union men. They were unruly, murdering thieves who ranged around Kansas and Missouri in guerrilla bands. The term jayhawking became a widely used synonym for stealing, but it did not carry a social stigma. Some important leaders were associated with jayhawking, such as James Henry Lane, who served in both the U.S. House of Representatives and the Senate.

Who were the fire-eaters

The Northerners used this term to describe Southern proslavery extremists before the Civil War. The most notable fire-eaters were Edmund Ruffin, Robert B. Rhett, and William L. Yancey. At a Tennessee convention, in 1820, the "fire-eaters" urged the South to secede (withdraw from the union) but this didn't occur for another ten years.

Where did guerrilla fighting start

In May 1861, Captain R.C.W. Radford from Virginia wrote to General Robert E. Lee. He offered to raise and equip a company of 1,000 active men for an irregular army if the Confederate government would arm them with long-range guns and pistols. Men were urged to form into companies for guerrilla warfare. Virginia started and Maryland, Alabama, followed by other Confederate states.

LIFE AS A SLAVE

As white politicians argued about slavery, black slaves lived miserable lives. Besides being made to work for nothing they were fed little, given poor clothing, lived in awful accommodations, and denied an education. Slaves were treated as property and not as human beings.

How did slaves live

Many slaves lived on plantations where they planted and harvested crops such as tobacco. Others lived in towns and cities, working in shops, hotels, and on small farms. They worked in the fields, and they often learned skilled trades, working as carpenters, blacksmiths and builders. Some slaves worked in mines and mills and as servants. The slave's life was not a happy one—many were tortured, sold and separated from their families.

How were slaves kept

Slaves had to work and live according to their master's rules. They were forced to work without pay and without the freedom to leave, considered as property, not human beings. Owners were allowed to beat their slaves and punish them severely. If they attempted to run away, they were forced to wear iron slave collars with three protruding long prongs. These collars were used to punish and identify slaves who were considered to be possible or risky runaways.

FACT BYTES

Following a slave auction, those slaves who were too sick to be of service were simply left to die after the auction was over.

How were slaves auctioned

When the ships with the slaves arrived, a gun would sound, and buyers and spectators would gather around for the auction. They were brought in individually and inspected like animals. Slaves who were not bought, due to illness, were known as "refuse." When the bid was agreed, the doors of the auction yard were opened, and a hoard of buyers would rush in to grab any "refuse" slaves.

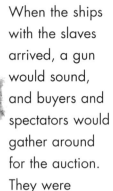

Slaves often worked in fields as cotton pickers.

Why were some angry about slave abolition

The South was an agricultural society. The Southerners needed slaves to work and tend their land. Without slaves, they wouldn't have the same level of wealth and prosperity. Owning slaves ensured the success of their futures and industry, because their land could continue to be maintained and developed. The abolition of slavery would take away their private property, their lifestyle and their industry, provoking fear.

What was the Fugitive Slave Act

Southern congressman passed this act to stop slaves escaping and to keep citizens from assisting in their escapes. These laws stated that it was illegal for anyone to help an escaped slave. The law demanded that if escaped slaves were sighted, they should be captured and turned in to the authorities for deportation back to the "rightful" Southern owner. The Fugitive Slave Act was so severe that it was ruled that any United States Marshall who refused to return a runaway slave would pay a penalty of $1,000.

LIFE AS A SLAVE

ABRAHAM LINCOLN

Abraham Lincoln is one of the most well known presidents in American history. His election as president in 1860 was met with controversy. Pro-slavery voters were outraged that a man opposed to slavery had been elected, and so disquiet and unrest swept through the Southern states.

Why was the 1860 election important

Abraham Lincoln.

A greater wedge of separation was growing between the North and the South because of the slavery issue, and consequently, leading to the threat of secession. (see pages 8-9). The results of the election could easily dictate the nation's future. If the South's proslavery candidate won, then secession might possibly be postponed or dismissed; however, if the North's anti-slavery candidate won, then secession would be probable or highly likely, and the course of the nation's future would be drastically altered.

What did Lincoln say about slavery

Abraham Lincoln opposed slavery. He was not an abolitionist, but he regarded slavery as an evil injustice, believing it to be unconstitutional and inhumane. Lincoln's parents were anti-slavery, and Lincoln adopted his parents' way of thinking. He said, "If slavery is not wrong, nothing is wrong. I cannot remember when I did not so think and feel." Lincoln stood by this viewpoint for most of his political career.

Abraham Lincoln delivering his famous speech at the battlefield of Gettysburg, on November 19, 1863.

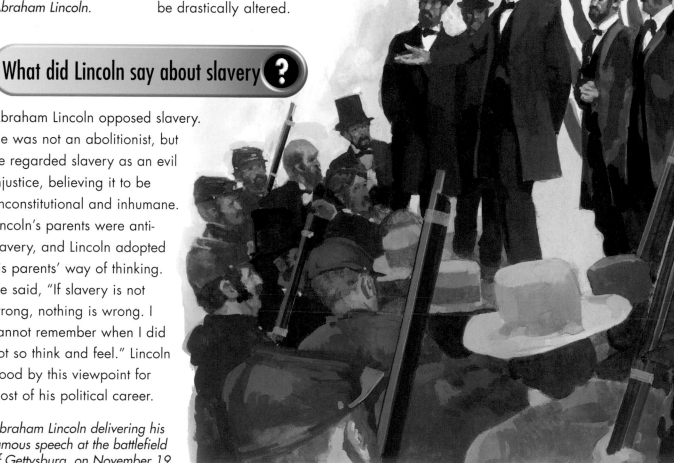

What were the election results

Stephen A. Douglas.

The election results were:

- Abraham Lincoln 180 electoral votes and 1,865,593 popular votes.
- Stephen A. Douglas Northern Democratic party 12 electoral votes and 1,382,713 popular votes.
- John C. Breckinridge Southern Independent Democratic party 72 electoral votes and 848,356 popular votes.
- John Bell Constitutional Union 39 electoral votes and 592,906 popular votes.

What were the consequences of Lincoln's unexpected victory

Lincoln's election, together with the secession crisis, acted as the immediate trigger for the Civil War itself. The South highly opposed Lincoln's view on slavery and feared for their future. Upset by his victory, they fervently strived to preserve their institution of slavery despite his political stance. The fall of the Democrats and election of Lincoln provided the fire-eaters with the momentum they needed to lead the Lower South into secession in the winter of 1860 and 1861.

Lincoln celebrating his victory.

What famous speech did Abraham Lincoln deliver on November 19, 1863

After the war had ended, Lincoln delivered a two-minute Gettysburg Address at a ceremony dedicating the Battlefield as a National Cemetery on November 19, 1863. Lincoln gave this speech at the site of the bloody July 1-3, 1863 Civil War battle in Gettysburg, Pennsylvania. It was a heartfelt speech that stated President Lincoln's feelings about the war and the country. In this speech, Lincoln conveyed his feelings about unity and fighting for a cause. This speech has been acclaimed as one of the most significant and memorable speeches of the Civil War.

ABRAHAM LINCOLN

SECESSION

After the election of Abraham Lincoln as president, many Southerners were afraid that they would lose their voice in American government, and the right to own slaves. South Carolina's voters called for secession from the Union and declared their independence in December, 1860, an act that would ultimately lead to the first shots of the Civil War.

What was secession

Secession is the act of withdrawing from an organized body or union. The South was a part of the Union but didn't agree with the leadership's political views on slavery and wanted to "secede." As slavery was such an important issue in their industry and lifestyle, they believed that they should operate under a different entity to ensure their financial success and future livelihood. The South, therefore, formed their own union, or "Confederacy."

What happened in Charleston, South Carolina

South Carolina was one state electing to secede from the Union, but there was still a question of who controlled the military posts. Fort Sumter, in Charleston Harbor, was a garrison in question. Abraham Lincoln sent relief there, sensing possible attack. This encouraged the South to bombard, creating the first engagement of the Civil War.

Fort Sumter.

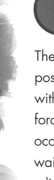

Who surrounded Fort Sumter

The Confederates waited for the Union to clear the post so they could be in control, arming themselves with guns that covered the harbor entrances. Their forces and strength outweighed those of the Union occupying the fort at that time. The Confederacy were waiting in the harbor to deter the Union from sending relief and reinforcement, ready to fire if they saw any signs of the Union attempting to send aid.

Who fired the first shots of the American Civil War

The Confederates fired the first shots of the war at Fort Sumter. On February 18, Jefferson Davis sent a diplomatic mission to Washington seeking Union removal of the garrison there. On March 4, Lincoln was sworn in and decided to reinforce the fort. Upon hearing this, Confederate officials placed their men on alert. On April 11, they demanded that the fort's commander, Anderson surrender. He declined, saying he was short on supplies and would probably leave soon. The Confederates issued a deadline for him to be gone but he failed, so Southern troops opened fire.

Who was Jefferson Davis

Jefferson Davis was an American soldier and politician, who attended the United States Military Academy at West Point and graduated as a Second Lieutenant. He married Miss Knox Taylor, and both he and she contracted malaria shortly after their marriage. He recovered, but he lost his wife after only three months of marriage. He never served a full term in any elected office, including the Presidency.

Jefferson Davis.

Who formed the Confederate States of America

FACT BYTES

Inside the Charleston secession hall was the actual place where state representatives voted for separation from the Union.

The Confederate States of America was the government formed by the states that seceded from the Union, and was formed on February 18, 1861. Jefferson Davis was their president. It comprised the following states: South Carolina, Mississippi, Florida, Alabama, Georgia, Louisiana, Texas, Virginia, Arkansas, Tennessee, and North Carolina.

THE RISE OF THE ARMIES

In 1861, after the Confederate army captured Fort Sumpter, Abraham Lincoln began to mobilize the Union's army in preparation for war. Loyal state governors sent 75,000 troops to protect Washington D.C. In the South, Jefferson Davis recruited 100,000 volunteers and prepared to attack.

What is conscription

A conscription poster.

Some countries legally require that their citizens serve a term in their armed forces. This process is generally known as conscription. Most countries only draft men, but some also draft women. The only time "the draft" is used is during wartime, because during other times, the countries rely on their volunteers or professional military forces.

Who volunteered for the armies

The Union military comprised men from the United States, Germany, Ireland, France, Spain, Great Britain and Italy, and signed up 16,000 men for five years. On April 15, 1861, President Lincoln pleaded for 75,000 volunteers to serve for ninety days. As the war continued and the volunteers stopped joining the army, the government offered money to volunteers. The Southern soldiers were called Rebels. In the beginning, the Southern forces consisted of small state units. President Jefferson Davis asked for 100,000 volunteers.

Volunteers queuing.

FACT BYTES

If a man owned twenty or more slaves, he didn't have to fight. Officers were paid significantly better wages than any normal soldier.

How many soldiers were drafted in

Under the Union draft act, men faced possible conscription in July 1863 and in March, July, and December of 1864. In the Union, of the 249,259 18-to-35-year-old men whose names were drawn, only about six per cent served. In the Confederacy, The Conscription Act of February 1864 called all men between the age of seventeen and fifty. Conscripts accounted for one-fourth to one-third of the Confederate armies east of the Mississippi between April of 1864 and early 1865. Not everyone agreed to the draft with both Northern and Southern protesting against it. There were even riots against the conscription.

A young conscripted soldier.

Guns and wagons stuck in mud.

How much were soldiers paid

The Union initially paid their soldiers $13, and the Confederacy initially paid theirs $11. Later, soldiers' pay was raised to $16 in the North and $18 in the South. At that time, a typical laborer made about $30 a month. Union soldiers were supposed to be paid every two months in the field, but there were times when they went eight months without. The Confederate army pay was even slower and less regular.

When did the armies fight

Moving armies in rainy weather was extremely difficult and often impossible. The rain would turn the dusty roads into mud, and the soldiers' feet and horses' hooves churned the mud to a thick, heavy bog. The big guns and wagons would get stuck in the mud fairly quickly. The armies also tried to avoid fighting in winter. The snow and rain would only bog down the wagon trains, so most of the Civil War battles occurred in the summer weather rather than in the winter. Most Civil War soldiers spent their winter months in camp.

THE RISE OF THE ARMIES

MULTINATIONAL FORCES

Many different nationalities were recruited into the Union and Confederate armies during the Civil War. There was a great deal of prejudice against immigrant groups and ethnic minorities so many of these men established their own volunteer regiments.

Who did the Native Americans fight for ?

Almost 12,000 Native Americans served in the Confederate army. The numbers were far less for the North which had about 3,500. At the outbreak of the Civil War, the minority party gave its allegiance to the Confederacy, while the majority party helped the North. Several hundred Mexican-Americans joined up in the west, namely Colorado, New Mexico, and Texas. However, many Native Americans were treated subclass on both sides, and defection was common.

Which nationalities were involved ?

Based on enlistment rolls and other official reports, out of approximately 2,000,000 Union soldiers enlisted during the war, over two-thirds were native born Americans. Therefore, only under one-third of all troops were non-natives and included Germans, Irish, British, Canadians, French, Italians, Poles, Scandinavians, Scottish, Mexicans, and Jews. These nationalities formed regiments to defend the Union, because they felt loyalty for the opportunities that had been afforded them. Many supported the Republican party, but some, such as the Irish, stood behind the Democratic party.

Who was Colonel Marcus M. Spiegel

Marcus M. Spiegel was one of the few Jewish generals during the Civil War. He served two and a half years in the Union army. He arrived in America from Germany twelve years prior to the Civil War and acquired a great command of the English language. He was an ardent patriot and devoutly religious man who fought for the Union's cause. He was an eternal optimist who recorded the events of his life in the army in writing. He led the 120th regiment with total loyalty and patriotism to the Union and its cause.

Why did Canadians fight in the Civil War

Canadians who fought in the war did so for a variety of reasons. Some fought voluntarily, while others were pressed into service by shady recruiting tactics called crimping. Many Canadians found themselves to be fighting for their "adopted country," having left Canada to reside in the states at some time in their lives. Many of these came when they were young. It is believed that thousands of Canadians served during the Civil War. Most of them likely came from the then independent Maritime provinces and Canada East which is now known as Quebec.

Soldiers from Great Britain marching to fight for the Union army.

FACT BYTES

Some people formed their own volunteer regiments. By 1863, New York and Pennsylvania had each provided over 170 regiments of infantry to the Union cause with Ohio, Indiana, Massachusetts, Connecticut, Maine, and Illinois following close behind. Southern states raised and supplied the Confederate armies with volunteer regiments, too.

MULTINATIONAL FORCES

EQUIPPING ARMIES

Armies have to be well provided with clothing and equipment if they are to be effective in war. During the American Civil War, factories in the Northern states provided the army with plentiful supplies. In the Southern states there were less factories and soldiers often had to make their own uniforms and carried imported weapons.

How were the soldiers dressed

Union soldiers wore uniforms of dark blue coats, light blue pants, and a cap (kepi) with a round, flat crown, and a visor. Southerners wore similar uniforms with gray jackets and light blue pants. The soldiers preferred shoes that had broad bottoms and big, flat heels, instead of heavy boots that were difficult to put on and take off, especially when wet. Soldiers were ill-fitted and poorly clothed, and often times Confederate soldiers would even have to go barefoot, because they didn't have the benefits of the shoe-making industry in the North.

What did the factories produce

The factories of the North produced clothing, firearms, shoes, and locomotives which gave them a distinct advantage. By the onset of the Civil War, the Confederate states had factories that produced 100 rifles per day as compared to the 38 Union arms factories that were capable of producing a total of 5,000 infantry rifles per day.

What was a butternut

Since individual soldiers had to pay out of their own pockets for clothing issued that was in excess of their given allotment, they wanted to wear what they had for as long as possible. Confederate troops needed to be outfitted with a mix of varying shades of gray and butternut along with some sky blue pants. Many of the gray dyes used at that time faded to butternut, so as the war continued, the uniforms shifted from predominately gray to this colour, as the North slowly reduced the South's ability to supply its armies with clothes.

Which armies were better supplied

The Union army was better supplied than the Confederate army. The North had the industrial resources to produce the weapons of war. The Northern mines produced the iron that was molded into cannons and used for ironclad ships. There was only one place in the South that could manufacture cannons. There was only one small mill that was able to manufacture gunpowder for the entire Confederate army. Because of this, the Union armies had more weaponry, and they were better equipped to fight in the war.

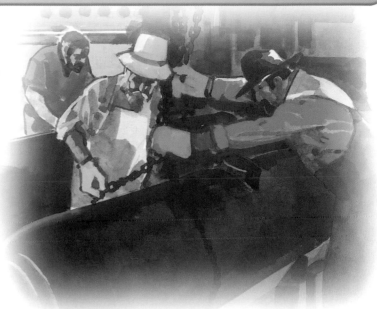

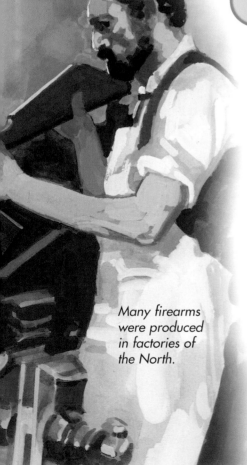

Many firearms were produced in factories of the North.

Why were uniforms scarce for Southern soldiers

Although the South produced cotton, they sent almost all their cotton to Europe or the Northern states to be manufactured into cloth. They did this prior to the Civil War. There weren't any factories to manufacture uniforms. The women in the South had to learn from their grandmothers or from their poorer neighbors how to weave homespun cloth. They made dye for this cloth from the butternuts, and this is how the Confederate uniform came to be a warm brown color of butternut, rather than gray.

FACT BYTES

Even though the South flourished in raising cotton, the North was more equipped to produce it and therefore profited from its production.

A woman works on a piece of butternut-dyed cloth.

EQUIPPING ARMIES

WEAPONS OF WAR

At the beginning of the Civil War the armies fought with old-fashioned infantry charges and cavalry attacks. By the war's end, weapons of great firepower were being used. The soldiers' weapons ranged from guns, knives, and swords for personal combat to large cannons for battlefield combat.

What is an Enfield rifle

British Enfield rifles.

The British Enfield rifle was the second most widely used weapon of the Civil War. It was a three-band, single-shot, muzzle-loading musket and was also the standard weapon for the British army between 1853-1867. American soldiers liked it because its .577 caliber barrel allowed the use of .58 caliber ammunition which was used by both the Union and Confederate armies. However, many officers preferred the Springfield muskets over the Einfelds primarily because of the interchangeability of parts that the machine-made Springfields offered.

How were the guns loaded

To load a muzzle-loading rifle, one had to follow these 10 specific steps to prepare it to fire: (1) lower the musket to the ground, (2) handle the cartridge, (3) tear the cartridge, (4) charge the cartridge, (5) draw the rammer, (6) ram the cartridge twice, (7) return the rammer, (8) cast-about [return the gun to firing position], (9) prime [insert the primer cap, (10) cock the hammer and then, point the rifle. They expected trained soldiers to complete these steps in 20 seconds as well as be able to fire three aimed bullets per minute.

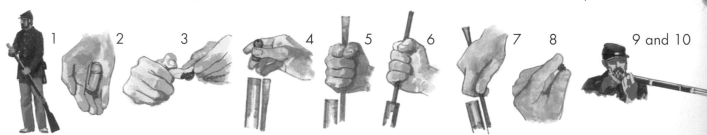

1   2   3   4   5   6   7   8   9 and 10

Why was a Henry rifle called a repeater

The Henry played an important role during the Civil War especially in the western theater. It was used from the very beginning to the tragic end of the Civil War. The soldiers developed confidence when they used their Henrys that didn't exist with a muzzle loader. The Henry rifle was the first of the genuinely rapid fire small arms that was practical. It had a lever acting, tube loading repeater, and this made its power equivalent to the current single shot rifles.

FACT BYTES

Mini balls could reach a half-mile or more, and an average soldier could easily hit a target that was 250 yards away.

A Union soldier in uniform.

Why were swords used

Swords were only used regularly in the cavalry, and generally only at the beginning of the war. They became marks of rank and in the later years were abandoned in favor of more efficient and sophisticated weapons. Sword charges stood little chance of success in the last years of the war against veteran soldiers who were armed with modern weapons fighting from concealed positions. Until recent years in America, swords were the symbol of an officer's authority, and this was their primary function in the Civil War.

What did a soldier carry

The soldiers were loaded down with fifty or sixty pounds of heavy equipment. Their guns could weigh up to fifteen pounds, and their knapsacks or haversacks could weigh as much as twenty pounds. Some soldiers marched in troops that carried all they possessed with them, while others marched with only their musket, ammunition, knapsack, haversack, and canteen, allowing them to be in trim for working or fighting. The soldiers would also carry their shoulder arms, small arms, and swords if they had them.

How were bullets made

The Minie ball was the standard bullet of the war and was made from very soft lead. French army Captain Claude F. Minie was the creator of this smaller, hollow-based bullet that could quickly and easily be rammed into the bore. It expanded when the weapon was fired and spun when it was shot out of the barrel. That spin made the mini ball bullet a highly precise and far traveling projectile.

French army Captain Claude F. Minie.

WEAPONS OF WAR

17

WAR WOMEN

Women were prohibited from fighting during the Civil War, but they were allowed to contribute to the war effort in other ways. When men went off to war, women were left to look after things at home and had to do work that was traditionally done by men.

Why couldn't women fight

At that time, there existed Victorian social constraints and beliefs, demanding that a woman's place was in the home. Women were confined to the domestic sphere of life, and both the Confederate and Union armies forbade the enlistment of female soldiers. During that time period, women were expected to accept their dictated societal role, and they were believed to be frail, submissive, passive human beings who had no interest in the political, military, or public life.

How did women help

Women helped in many different ways. Some women worked as nurses to the soldiers, while some stayed home and maintained the homefront while their husbands were off at war. Others served as romantic spies for their side, and some served as laundresses doing laundry for the military men. Others helped teach soldiers to read and write, and more would help clean and load the muskets. Many women joined Women's Relief Societies to help aid the soldiers in need.

Who was Loreta Janeta Velazquez

Loreta Janeta Velazquez (left) published a book called *The Woman in Battle* in 1876, where she tells of how she disguised herself as a male soldier and served in battle. She claimed that she assumed the name of Harry T. Buford and that she wore a fake moustache, developed a masculine walk, learned to smoke a cigar, and padded her uniform so that she appeared like a muscular man. Many scholars deny the authenticity of her story; however, others feel that much of what she wrote depicts the time period most accurately. She claimed four marriages but never took on any of her husbands' names. She was a widow when she claimed to have enlisted as a soldier.

Who was Clara Barton

Clara Barton was an intelligent woman who initially served as Superintendent of Nurses during the Civil War period. After the war, President Lincoln gave her permission to begin a letter writing campaign to find missing soldiers. She worked so hard that she became physically exhausted, so she followed her doctor's orders and went to Europe for rest. There, she learned of the Treaty of Geneva and the Red Cross that provided relief for wounded and sick soldiers. She came back and pleaded that the Union sign the treaty. At first, the Union refused to sign the treaty. However, due to her dedicated lobbying, the American Red Cross organization was formed in 1881, and she served as its first president.

Clara Barton.

What was the sanitary commission

The official warrant creating this commission was issued by the War Department on June 9, 1861. At that time, there were many women's relief societies; however, there wasn't much organization or direction. The Sanitary Commission provided sanctions and guidelines as to how nursing care would be given, how hospitals would be organized, and how dietary and health safety precautions would be followed. The Sanitary Commission delegates would communicate regularly with the Medical Bureau and The War Department concerning these areas and guidelines.

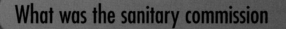

Many women worked as nurses.

FACT BYTES

Some women disguised themselves as soldiers, and fought on the battlefield. By assuming masculine names, binding their breasts, padding the waists of their trousers, and cutting their hair short, women could easily pass for male soldiers.

WAR WOMEN

BLACK VOLUNTEERS

Approximately 180,000 African-Americans comprising 163 units served in the Union Army during the Civil War, and many more served in the Union Navy. Many white soldiers and officers believed that black men lacked the courage to fight but the black soldiers soon proved their capability and many won the Medal of Honour.

Who did black soldiers fight for

The black soldiers fought for both the Union and the Confederacy. By the end of the war, one-tenth of the Union army was black. Although the Confederate Congress didn't authorize all-black Units in the Confederate Army until it was too late, in 1865, there were an estimated 50,000 African-Confederates unofficial black soldiers who served for them.

Why is Col. Robert Gould Shaw remembered

Robert Gould Shaw is the brave colonel who led the 54th Massachusetts in their fearless charge at Fort Wagner. Shaw was passionately opposed to slavery. When he was asked to command the Massachusetts Fifty-Fourth Regiment in February of 1863, his dealings with black people had been more theoretical than actual. When the South discovered this black regiment had been formed, they were outraged. They threatened to execute any white officer of this troop—so Shaw placed himself in the front lines of battle and died, taking a shot through the heart.

How did the Emancipation Proclamation help slaves

On January 1,1863, President Abraham Lincoln declared that all slaves residing in territory rebelling against the federal government should be freed. This Emancipation Proclamation freed few slaves, because it didn't apply to those in border states fighting on the Union side, and it didn't affect slaves in southern areas that were already under Union control. The rebelling states didn't follow the President's orders; but it did confirm the abolition of slavery as a major war goal.

How were prejudices overcome in the army

Initially, the United States government had no intent to enlist black men. However, after a year of fighting, and the consistent plea by blacks to take part, the government discovered it needed them and was forced to rethink its recruitment policy. After allowing black men to enlist, their troops had many successes in combat, thus creating a more positive northern public opinion of black soldiers. The New York Tribune stated, "Facts are beginning to dispel prejudices." When Lincoln discovered the success of the black troops, he urged the white commanders to use them whenever possible.

What did black soldiers do in the army

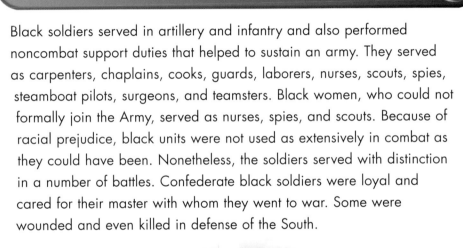

Black soldiers served in artillery and infantry and also performed noncombat support duties that helped to sustain an army. They served as carpenters, chaplains, cooks, guards, laborers, nurses, scouts, spies, steamboat pilots, surgeons, and teamsters. Black women, who could not formally join the Army, served as nurses, spies, and scouts. Because of racial prejudice, black units were not used as extensively in combat as they could have been. Nonetheless, the soldiers served with distinction in a number of battles. Confederate black soldiers were loyal and cared for their master with whom they went to war. Some were wounded and even killed in defense of the South.

Left: Many black men served in both armies during the Civil War.

Right: Some black men worked as tradesmen.

BLACK VOLUNTEERS

THE BATTLE OF BULL RUN

Bull Run was the first major battle of the Civil War and was fought in Virginia, near the Manassas, Virginia railway junction. The armies in this first battle were not very large by later Civil War standards. The Union forces were organised into four divisions of about 30,000 men. The Confederate command structure was somewhat more unwieldy, including two "armies," with no division structure and thirteen independent brigades.

Why did the battle take place

Union soldiers.

After the firing of the first gun at Fort Sumter, both the North and the South began lining up their forces on a line (Bull Run-stream) along the border states from the Atlantic coast of Virginia to Kansas in the west. The South was pushing secession, and the North was attempting to hold the Union together. Fort Sumter caused a chain of events including the burning of bridges and cut-off railway communication between Washington and the North. The North was hurting and fearing secession of more states. Both the North and South were trying to obtain control of these states to fight for their side.

Why was it important ?

This battle would set the tone and help to predict what the possible outcome of the war would be. If the South won, their confidence would be boosted and give them momentum to continue their fight for secession and a government of their own. If the North won, they, too, would develop confidence and gain momentum to keep the Union together and hinder the South from causing more division and separation of the Union. Some thought this would be the only battle of the War, but it was only the beginning.

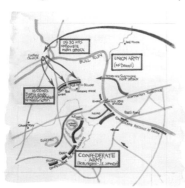

Union soldiers (left) bear the Union flag whilst confederates (right) proudly defend their own standard.

FACT BYTES

The principal commanders in the battle of Bull Run were Brigadier General Irvin McDowell (left) (Union), Brigadier General Joseph E. Johnston (Confederacy), and Brigadier General P.G.T. Beauregard also from the Confederacy.

Why was there panic on the roads ?

At first when the Union withdrew and retreated, it was orderly, but when the federal troops found the roads jammed with spectators of civilians and congressmen, they fled back to the defenses of Washington. The short battle had turned into a full-blown war and they were ridden with fear and despair. The sight of more people and the chaos of the moment simply added to their upset, and the roads were filled with panic.

What happened ?

On July 16, 1861, General McDowell marched his untried troops from Washington against the Confederate army which was lined up behind Bull Run. On July 21, General McDowell crossed at Sudley Ford and attacked the Confederate left flank on Matthews Hill. Fighting continued and raged on throughout the day. The Confederacy was much more prepared for fighting than the Union. Confederate reinforcements extended, and they were able to break the Union right flank. The Union forces had to retreat and were forced to leave.

How was the battle won ?

The Union forces were tired and unprepared for war. The Confederates were close in proximity and were refreshed and prepared for battle. When they were able to break the Union right flank, the Union forces had to retreat and were forced to leave. The South had won the battle; however, although they were the victors, they were too disorganized to continue their pursuit. As a result, Confederate General Bee and Colonel Bartow were killed as Thomas J. Jackson stood there like a "stonewall", earning his nickname.

Thomas J. Jackson.

THE BATTLE OF BULL RUN

23

LIFE IN THE ARMY

Soldiers spent most of their time outdoors, all year round. During campaigns, most men had to sleep on the ground covered with a blanket but in the winter, when fighting wasn't common, they would sometimes build simple wooden barracks.

Where did soldiers sleep

Soldiers slept on the hard ground.

The soldiers slept on the ground or beds of straw covered with blankets. The ground was often cold and damp. Sometimes they would sleep with another blanket that covered their bodies. Some slept in open tents that were made from muslin stretched over three-foot poles. If it rained, the water beat in on them, and the wind also hit them severely, because there were no closed sides to protect them. Bugs and creepy crawlies would crawl all over them, and mosquitoes often bit them. They wore heavy woollen clothing that caused them to perspire from a long day's work. So, when they went to retire for the evening, they became chilled from the dampness of their clothes.

What did soldiers eat ?

The soldiers ate whatever was made available to them. As they were hungry, they were grateful for any food. Sometimes, they ate meat and potatoes and bread. At others they would eat pork and beans. These rations were not all served out at one time. They would be given single rations, including portions of the items shown below. Sometimes they would even have to eat maggoty food and hardtack.

A resting soldier.

FACT BYTES

A soldier's diet might have included salt pork, fresh beef, salt beef, bread, potatoes, beans, split peas, rice, dried apple, dried peaches, coffee, tea, sugar, molasses, and an occasional onion.

Soldiers building their barracks.

How did they spend their free time

The soldiers participated in rough sports, decorated their winter quarters like the comforts of home and sang romantic songs. Some went to religious meetings and revivals, and on picnics whenever they were allowed. They wrote letters to their loved ones, and played any game they could create, including baseball and cards. They even held boxing matches, and cockfights. Some soldiers raced lice or cockroaches across a strip of canvas. Others played the guitar, the banjo, or the fiddle.

When did they build barracks

As soon as the soldiers arrived at the site where it had been decided they would set up camp, they began building their barracks. Every company was expected to build its own quarters and this kept soldiers busy when they were not in combat. Hundreds of men would carry boards on their shoulders and work hard to build. Others would dig ditches while still others cooked. All of the soldiers stayed busy, diligently working to make themselves comfortable.

What did the old and young do

Most of the Civil War soldiers were between the ages of 18 and 30. However, there were some boys and older men who carried rifles. Many of them came from rural areas, did not have much education, and had never been far from home. Despite its horrors and hardships, fighting in the war was the greatest adventure of their lives. The young men were anxious to prove their masculinity, so the thought of fighting for their side was appealing and honorable. They felt like they were transforming from "boys" to "men." Older generals and commanders would lead the troops.

A young soldier.

ARTILLERY

During the American Civil War more varieties of projectiles and cannons were used than in any other time in military history. The outbreak of hostilities in 1861, found inventors on both sides searching for the perfect blend of sabot, shell body, and fuse to create the artillery that would give their military an advantage.

Why were cannons so effective

During the Civil War, the North created the largest cannons that were ever produced. The cannons were made on a round track so they could rotate in a circular motion. This gave them the ability of being able to shoot at multiple angles, an advantage in a war situation. As they weren't portable, they were basically used in forts as defense mechanisms. Cannons made it impossible for important forts to be penetrated, and this was a definite advantage in their defense and protection.

A cannon on a round track to improve its range.

How were cannons loaded ?

The barrels had to be inspected to make sure they were clean and empty. After firing, the soldiers had to wait several minutes before firing again. They had to insert a piece of fuse all the way into the vent hole and bend it at the top so it was perpendicular to the hole. Then, they had to determine the correct amount of black powder to use based on the bore diameter. Next, they poured the powder into the barrel. They would then check around the area to make certain it was clear, before announcing for it to be fired. The person firing it would light the fuse and retreat.

FACT BYTES

Solid shot and shell ammunition were used against long-range, fixed targets such as forts. Chain shot, comprising two balls connected by a chain, was used against masts and rigging of ships.

How heavy were cannonballs

Cannonballs weighed between 12 and 90 pounds. Artillery ammunition included grape, canister, shell, solid shot, and chain shot. Canister was a scattershot projectile of small iron balls in a container. They were packed in a tin can while grape shot was usually wrapped in a canvas or cloth covering and tied with string that made it look like a bunch of grapes. The can or wrapping disintegrated upon firing and released the shot in a spray.

Shell shot.

Canister shot.

Solid shot.

Chain shot.

How were they moved around

The cannons had carriages which served numerous functions. One function they served was that of mobility. The carriage of the cannon allowed it to be easily moved where needed. It had wheels which allowed it to roll on the ground and move from place to place. The carriages also had caissons that held ammunition chests and enabled them to carry their ammunition along with the artillery itself. Artillery horses would pull the carriages that contained the heavy mounted artillery, and drivers were needed to steer the horses.

How did cannons work

A smooth-bored cannon.

There were two types of cannon—the smooth-bored and rifled. They were either ignited by the flash of the discharge, or fired by the impact of the projectile striking the target which was called percussion. Smooth-bored cannons used the timed fuse, and rifled cannons used both the timed and percussion. However, neither fuse was very good, because the black powder they used didn't burn at a reliable rate.

A rifled cannon.

HORSEMEN

Soldiers on horseback played an important role in the American Civil War. Amongst other duties, cavalry men scouted out enemy troops, made shock raids, charged down infantry on the battle field and acted as speedy messengers.

Why, and how, were horsemen effective

Union soldiers on horseback.

Initially, the horsemen served largely as scouts and escorts, but experience brought amazing changes. After a few battles in conjunction with the infantry, the horse soldiers began breaking away from their bases to destroy enemy communications and supplies. They burned stores and bridges, ripped out telegraph lines, and raided far behind the lines attempting to keep the enemy so busy that they could apply only limited potential when battle was joined.

What weapons did they carry

Horsemen carried breech loading rifles, pistols, revolvers, and sabers. They wore sabers and belts, with the straps that pass over the shoulders, and carbines and slings and carried pocketfuls of cartridges as well as several models of breech-loading carbines. Later, came the Quickloader, which enabled a trooper to fire a dozen aimed shots a minute. However, there were still many Southerners who argued, until long after the war, in favor of their old Enfields and Springfield rifles. These, they claimed were more accurate and of longer range than the newer Spencer or Sharp's carbines.

Union cavalryman (left and Confederate cavalryman (right).

What did the cavalrymen wear

The cavalry officers wore a yellow shoulder strap, a crimson sash, and a scarlet trouser welt. The enlisted cavalry men wore a yellow welt on the collar, a yellow hat cord, a yellow chevron, and yellow NCO pants. They wore jackets as opposed to frock coats. The Regulations called for cavalry men's hats to be looped on the right (sword arm) side.

Horse riding was second nature to those brought up in the South.

Which side had the strongest cavalry ?

Initially, the South had a distinct advantage when it came to the cavalry. Southern men from early childhood were accustomed to the outdoor life and rode almost everywhere. The elite cavalry units of the Confederate army attracted many of the sons of aristocratic planters who would rather fight in the saddle as a private, than lead men by foot as an officer. The Union mounted forces were initially swept from the field by the more skilled Southern riders; however, in time, the Union's cavalry grew stronger, forcing more battles to be fought dismounted.

What was the largest "all cavalry" battle ?

The largest "all cavalry" battle of the war was fought at Trevilian Station in 1864. Here, the Northern and Southern horsemen fought each other to a standstill. As the Union cavalry became more expert at fighting mounted, the advantage of mounted combat for the South decreased, and the Confederate horsemen fought more and more on foot. During this battle, a large amount of both forces were dismounted. Both the 7th Virginia and the 1st Connecticut fought in the battle at Trevilian Station.

FACT BYTES

Mounted Union cavalrymen wore a carbine sling across their chests, and the carbine barrel peeked from behind their right leg. A cavalry saber and scabbard was worn on the left of their body.

Their trousers had a one-half inch stripe down over the outer seam. Many horse-riding soldiers wore knee-high leather boots which offered protection to their lower leg.

The Union cavalry preparing to charge.

HORSEMEN

LIFE IN THE NORTH

Many people in the Northern states were shocked when the the Southern states decided to leave the Union, and absolutely outraged when they fired at Fort Sumpter. The Union success during the Civil War was built on the success of the factories on the home front in the North.

How did life change during the war ?

The North suffered casualties, but they had become stronger and richer than ever before. Their industry helped them during the war. Owners of factories made money selling guns, clothes, wagons, and tents to the army. Thousands of new immigrants poured in from  Europe, and new railroads united California and the east. Industry was booming! Despite the participation of women in the war, they had discovered that their positions and roles had really not changed. Although they entered the workplace to replace the soldiers who had gone to war, they were still not allowed to vote.

How did the Union grow larger and more wealthy ?

New railroads emerged during the Civil War.

As the union had to manufacture the weapons and materials to sustain the armies, industry was booming. Businesses were flourishing and thriving by meeting the demand for supplies. The more they manufactured, the more money they made, and the larger they grew. With time and experience, their products became more refined, adding to business growth and development. The war had created an increasing need for manufactured goods, and the union was prospering as a result of having to meet those demands.

What religious themes had a major impact on the North during the Civil War

Several religious themes had a major impact on the North during the Civil War, such as the belief that America was preparing the way for the kingdom of God on Earth, the conviction that blood needed to be shed in order for the nation to be reborn, and the churches' growing conviction that the hand of Providence was indicating the need to end slavery. Because of this latter belief, they embraced full emancipation as a war aim. The Protestant churches also were led to support the Radical Republicans during the Reconstruction because of their convictions on emancipation.

FACT BYTES

Steam-driven machinery helped the North to maintain a much more efficient manufacturing system. Southern states often relied upon natural power from running stream water.

How did Northern industry help win the war

Northern industry was a significant factor in securing the North's victory. Industry enabled the North to manufacture weapons and artillery as well as clothing and shoes to outfit the armies. No army could possibly be prepared to fight without supplies, and supplies had to be manufactured. The North was equipped to do this. While the South was suffering in agriculture, the North was prospering in industry. They also had more railroads which enabled them to move supplies, men, and equipment. They prospered in the banking and shipping industries too.

Railroads made the movement of supplies much easier.

Why did baseball grow in popularity

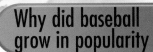

As there were a large number of young men in the armies, baseball, the sport that was once considered a game for "gentlemen" only, was converted into a game that was played by all ranks of army men to take their minds off the rigor and sorrow of war. Officers and enlisted men played side by side, and soldiers earned their positions on the team because of their athletic ability, not their social status or rank. As a result of this, it has been forever linked with patriotism.

LIFE IN THE NORTH

LIFE IN THE CONFEDERATE STATES

The Confederate States of America existed for only four years. During this time, the citizens of this nation established many of the institutions already existing in the Union, including a presidency, a House of Representatives and a Senate. They also printed their own currency, had their own flag and drafted a constitution very similar to that of the United States.

How did life change during the war ?

During the war, it became more difficult for Southern children to attend school. First, the tutors went to fight in the war. Then, the children had to help out on the farm or in the house, leaving them less time to study. Next, many schools were used as prisons or hospitals. Some families only ate one or two small meals a day to make the food last. Women and children had to do more chores while the men went off to fight.

Why did the Confederation economy suffer ?

The Confederation economy suffered, because they needed the industry of the North to sustain their way of living. Although they raised crops and cotton, they couldn't do this successfully without the aid from industry. Food and supplies were limited because the Union Army cut their railroad lines and the Union Navy blocked their ports. The foreign nations didn't even recognize them as a government, so trade was blocked with them.

Union Army cut their railroad lines.

Why did a lack of salt cost them dearly ?

Salt is essential in every human's diet, therefore, without it, the soldiers wouldn't be healthy enough to fight a war. Salt was also necessary for the horses and livestock and to preserve meat. It was also used to preserve leather during hide making. The South's salt supply resources were hit hard during the war, (due to their locations) allowing the Union to succeed in military strategy as a result.

Soldiers recovering in hosptal.

What was education like in the South during the Civil War

During the Civil War, it became more difficult for Southern children to go to school, for the same reasons as those in the North—their tutors were at war, and schools were used as hospitals or prisons. African-American children in the South were not taught to read or write. One such boy, Frederick Douglass, knew it was important to learn to be able to get a better job should he ever become free, so he secretly learned from local white boys. Some slaves who knew how to read and write taught other slaves in "pit schools." These schools were hidden holes in the ground so they would not be caught.

Nurses looked after the wounded soldiers.

FACT BYTES

As most of the battles were fought in the South, residents there experienced the most upheaval. Food and supplies were limited because the Union army cut the railroad lines and the Union Navy blocked the ports.

Due to a lack of salt, the cavalry horses in General Lee's army acquired a hoof and tongue disease. This also provided a major setback in the war.

What institutions did they set up

The South set up a constitution that was nearly structurally identical to that of the Union. They both had a preamble and seven articles. They both created a national president, a legislature that consisted of the Senate and the House of Representatives, and a court system. They set up a constitution that allowed the president to serve a term of six years and hold more executive power. They also allowed for more states' rights, encouraging states to have the freedom to make their own choices. They strictly upheld popular sovereignty. Unfortunately, foreign countries did not recognize them as a government, and they had poor relations with foreign powers.

The South formed their own government.

WAR ON THE WAVES

The navies from both sides played a big part in the Civil War. Many battles were fought along America's coasts and rivers as the armies sought control over the waterways. The navies changed the technology of warfare. The Civil War led to floating mines and world's first ironclad warship, the *CSS Virginia.*

How were the ships designed

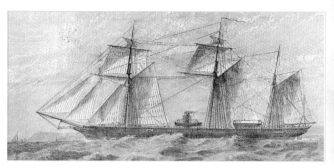

The CSS Alabama.

Some ships were lightweight schooners designed to travel quickly through narrow passages to run the blockades. The ships designed specifically for battle and combat included large, heavy, wooden ships, equipped with a large quantity of armament to engage in battles with weaponry. Others, known as ironclads, were designed to shoot within short ranges, and were often used close to shore.

How did the ships do battle

A floating mine.

The South would use their schooners to run blockades. When the North and South engaged in battles with weaponry, they would come up on their targets and begin shooting cannons. They also dropped floating mines in the water to destroy the enemy vessels. They also rammed with the ironclad vessels. As the South was at a distinct industrial disadvantage over the North, they had difficulty sustaining their naval battling abilities. They simply could not produce enough of the types of ships needed to engage in battles on the water.

FACT BYTES

Another highly successful development was the unusual-looking, double-ended gunboat, which was able to maneuver very well in narrow, twisting rivers.

Why was the *CSS Virginia* unique ❓

The *CSS Virginia* was formerly the *USS Merrimack*. This ship was seized by the Confederates in 1861 at Gosport Navy Yard and was then converted into an ironclad. The *CSS Virginia* engaged and sunk the *USS Cumberland* by ramming it. It then destroyed the *Congress* by fire. On March 9, 1862, it engaged the U.S. vessels *Monitor*, *Minnesota*, and *St. Lawrence*. It was run on shore near Craney Island and set on fire after being abandoned. It blew up at 4.58 a.m. on May 11, 1862.

The CSS Virginia.

Which battles were important ❓

The naval battle between the *USS Monitor* and the *CSS Virginia* was the first battle in history between steam-powered, ironclad ships with shell-firing guns. The North's naval blockade of the Confederate coast was one of the most aggressive up to that time. When the *CSS Nashville* ran the blockade out of Beaufort, North Carolina, this was known as the "Bull Run of the Navy." The battle of New Orleans and surrender of that city was another significant battle as was the battle of Galveston.

Navies on both sides of the conflict played an important role.

Why did Lincoln decide to blockade the Confederacy ❓

The only way the South could buy war supplies was to sell cotton to England and other European countries, so Lincoln decided to blockade the Confederacy. Northern ships would sail up and down the coast to stop the Southern ships from going in and out of the harbor. At the onset of the war, Lincoln only had ninety ships to patrol thousands of miles of coastline. Running the blockade became similar to a popular sport. By the conclusion of the war, the Union navy had 670 ships.

GUERRILLAS AND SABOTEURS

Civilians sometimes banded together to attack opposing troops and cause sabotage. Some people acted as spies, reporting the enemies military plans and strategies—something that was easy to do when the enemy spoke the same language and shared the same culture.

Who were the Partisan Rangers ?

A battle with the Blue Ridge Mountains in background.

The Partisan Rangers were irregular cavalrymen. They were not enlisted in the army by the government but formed independent units. Their purpose was to assist in the war without directly fighting in the line. They would make sudden dashes on the rear and flanks of the Union armies, or they would attack the Federal trains at night. They kept the outposts and train guard continuously on the alert.

How did people spy ?

People acted as undercover agents and crossed enemy lines with ease to retrieve information for their side. They often presented themselves to civilian and military officials, pumped them for information, and rode off with a cheerful good-bye. If the undercover spy simply paid attention to regional accents, the agent had little trouble disguising himself as a friend. Women often served as spies as well.

FACT BYTES

Spies would take newspaper articles that told of battle strategies from the oppositional side and deliver them to key people from their side to provide prior knowledge to outsmart the foe.

The South sometimes used booby traps to catch Northern spies crossing enemy lines by placing boards filled with sharp nails on the ground. When the enemy stepped on it, he would feel like he had stepped on a rake.

What happened to caught spies

Though spying and espionage was prevalent throughout the Civil War, and men and women who acted as undercover agents were masters at it, the consequences were severe should they be caught in the act. Spies who were discovered and exposed often faced execution. Many who were caught were hanged. The South sometimes used booby traps to catch Northern spies crossing enemy lines.

Spies, if caught, faced severe penalties such as hanging.

What weapons did they use

They used hot air balloons. These gave each side the opportunity of knowing where their enemies were. They would tie the balloons to a wench and send them up into the air. They had flags and would wave them in the direction of where their enemies were heading. Some of them also had the advantage of having a telegraph on board. The balloons were not easy to hit, because once in the sky, they were out of range of the cannons. They also used cannons, rifles, guns, and swords.

Both sides used hot air balloons.

Who was the Gray Ghost

The Gray Ghost was Confederate Colonel John Singleton Mosby. His group of Partisan Rangers was called Mosby's Rangers, and they disrupted enemy communication and supply lines. Although he was almost always outnumbered, he captured numerous men, supplies, information, and consistently destroyed many important railways. He would buy new uniforms and equipment for his men with the money he captured. He was extremely sneaky, and his night warfare tactics and supposed reported death on many occasions earned him the name "The Gray Ghost." Mosby always seemed to slip in without notice and wreak havoc on the enemy.

Colonel John Singleton Mosby (left).

GETTYSBURG

Of the more than 2,000 land engagements of the American Civil War, Gettysburg ranks supreme. Although the Battle of Gettysburg did not end the war, nor did it attain any major war aim for the North or the South, it remains the great battle and turning point of the war. More men fought and died on July 1, 2, and 3, 1863, at Gettysburg, than in any other battle before or since on North American soil.

What happened during this famous battle

Here, General Lee made his second attempt to invade the North. The Southern troops were ragged and had few supplies left, but they marched northward to the town of Gettysburg, Pennsylvania. Soldiers rode ahead to search for food and ran into Union cavalry. So the battle started by chance, but was still one of the bloodiest of the Civil War. By the second day of battle, the North was in possession of the high ground. There were two days of heavy Southern losses, when the South suffered 28,000 casualties. This was Lee's final invasion of the North, and it ended in defeat under the Union leadership of General Meade.

Why was the battle important

The battle caused thousands of casualties.

This battle was the turning point of the war. This was Lee's final invasion of the North, and thousands of casualties were suffered by the South. From then on, the war was fought in the fields and the cities of the South. The South would be the one to suffer the great losses—both in lives, land, territory, and buildings. This battle turned it around for the North, helping to ensure their final victory and the South's melancholy acceptance of defeat.

Union soldiers confront the Confederates at the battle of Gettysburg.

What happened at Little Round Top

Little Round Top was the most important part of the battlefield of Gettysburg. Had it been captured by the Confederates on the second day of battle, there wouldn't have been a third day or even a Union. The Union saw that this high ground (the unofficial high water mark) was undefended and sent their soldiers to the top. The Union received orders to hold the ground at all cost. After hours of fighting, the South had run out of ammunition. With no ammunition left, they were forced to leave and accept defeat.

What was the last Southern attack

Pickett's Charge was the last Southern attack, and every available soldier was used. Unfortunately for the South, the men had to charge uphill. At the top of the hill, Northern troops were kneeling behind stone fences and fired down on the masses of climbing men. Within one hour, 12,000 men fell. Those who managed to reach Union lines had to fight hand to hand with the Union troops. However, the Southerners didn't have any strength left. Northern reinforcements came and pushed the Confederates back to their own lines.

What famous commanders were involved

Some of the famous commanders involved in this battle were: General Robert E. Lee (left), Major General George C. Meade (below), General John F. Reynolds, Lieutenant General James Longstreet, Lieutenant General Richard S. Ewell, Major General Winfield S. Hancock, Brigadier General John B. Gordon, Major General Henry Heth, Colonel Joshua Chamberlain, Colonel Strong Vincent, Brigadier General Gouveneur K. Warren, Colonel E.P. Alexander, Major General George E. Pickett, and Brigadier General J.E.B. Stuart.

THE SIEGE OF VICKSBURG

The Confederacy had fortified Vicksburg, Mississippi, a town on the East bank of the Mississippi between Memphis, Tennessee, and New Orleans, Louisiana, and set up heavy artillery that could fire onto any vessel passing on the river. Vicksburg became one of the only places that kept the Mississippi river closed to Union traffic.

A map of Vicksburg.

Why was Vicksburg so vital ?

The North and South fought the war in the west for control of the rivers, especially the Mississippi. In addition to the gunboats, another great asset of the Union in the west was General Ulysses S. Grant. He besieged the city of Vicksburg, Mississippi for six weeks and starved the population into submission. With the Union now controlling the Mississippi River, the Confederacy became divided in two, and Texas, Louisiana, and Arkansas were now cut off from the other Southern states.

How was it won ?

General Grant realized that Vicksburg couldn't be taken by storm, so he decided to lay siege to the city. His army slowly established a line of works around Vicksburg, cutting it off from supply and communications with the outside world. He constructed several

approaches to destroy the Confederate defense line, detonated mines and aggressively bombarded the city with enemy guns, causing reduced rations of food and exposure to the elements. This caused starvation and weakness within the city. Vicksburg fell to the aggressive bombardment of the Union, and it had to accept defeat.

The seige of Vicksburg.

How were Ketchum hand grenades used

These were small explosive devices that were hand held and hand thrown. They were thrown like a dart, and would explode upon impact. There were one-, three-, and five-pounder grenades. When one of the forts was stormed, Confederate Captain John M. Hickey said, "The air was made black with hand grenades which were thrown at us by every Federal soldier who got inside the works." Many of these Ketchum grenades were recovered from the site of the Vicksburg battle.

A ketchum hand grenade.

What happened on Independence Day, July 4, 1863

General Grant offered parole instead of an unconditional surrender of the city and garrison to the courageous defenders of Vicksburg. Pemberton and his generals were in agreement that these were the best terms possible, and so the decision was made to surrender the city. On July 4, at 10:00 a.m., white flags were flown from the Confederate works, and the brave, fearless men in gray surrendered. Following this, the victorious Union army marched in and took control of the city.

Why was General Pemberton blamed

General Pemberton was a Northerner who had cast his lot in with the South. His wife was from Virginia, and influenced him. He was rebuked for surrendering at Vicksburg, and he eventually resigned from the army. Later, he volunteered to re-enlist as a private soldier. The South did not look favorably upon him and believed he was at fault for the surrender of Vicksburg. The real villain was probably the General Joe Johnston who had assembled 32,000 soldiers within a day's march of Vicksburg, yet he did not come to help. However, Pemberton was made the scapegoat.

General Pemberton.

FACT BYTES

When President Lincoln was informed about the fall of Vicksburg, he exclaimed, "The Father of Waters again goes unvexed to the sea."

THE SIEGE OF VICKSBURG

THE CONFEDERACY

On April 7, with the Confederate forces surrounded, Grant called upon Lee to surrender. On April 9, the two commanders met at Appomattox Courthouse, and agreed on the terms of surrender. This marked the formal end of the "War Between The States."

How were Sherman's troops decisive ?

Sherman's motive and goal was to literally march through Georgia and tear it apart. He was ordered by Grant to destroy the Southern countryside on which it depended for its supplies. Sherman and his troops marched through Georgia and set fire to farms, barns, and crops in the fields. Sherman said, "I can make Georgia howl!"

Events leading to the surrender of the Confederacy:

- Battle of Gettysburg.
- Siege of Vicksburg.
- Fall and abandonment of Atlanta.
- Re-election of Abraham Lincoln.
- Capturing of Savannah, Georgia.
- Fall of Nashville, Tennessee.
- Bombardment of Fort Fisher.
- General Sherman's destructive march from Georgia through South Carolina.
- Fall of Richmond, Virginia.
- Severe transportation problems, successful blockades.
- Surrender at Appomattox Courthouse.

Troops were ordered to destroy property in the state of Georgia.

What happened in Wilmer McLean's house ?

The house of Wilmer McLean.

General Lee went to see General Grant at the house of Wilmer McLean to discuss surrender terms, and it was here that Lee finally surrendered. McLean had lived near Manassas when a shell crashed through his kitchen roof during the first battle of Bull Run. He moved to Appomattox to escape from the war, but the final surrender of the Army of Northern Virginia happened in Mr. McLean's parlor, marking the official end of the Civil War.

Who assassinated Abraham Lincoln

John Wilkes Booth, born on May 10, 1838, was an actor, and also a racist and Southern sympathizer during the Civil War. Mr. Booth hated Abraham Lincoln and blamed him for all the South's problems. After Lincoln made a speech where he suggested that voting rights should be granted to certain blacks, Booth decided to pursue his assassination. When Lincoln came to the Ford theater to watch *Our American Cousin*, Booth was privy to his attendance and assassinated Abraham Lincoln.

John Wilkes Booth.

What happened to Jefferson Davis

After the fall of Petersburg, Jefferson Davis and his cabinet fled Richmond. Union troops captured Davis near Irwinville, Georgia. Davis planned to escape by sea along the eastern coast of Florida and sail to Texas where he hoped to establish a new Confederacy. On their way, the Cabinet disbanded and took payment from the gold of the treasury. Union soldiers found them and charged their camp. Davis and his family were taken to Fort Monroe, Virginia where he was imprisoned. Although he was indicted on the charge of treason, he was never tried and was released two years later.

What did the soldiers do afterwards

General Lee and the soldiers tried to hold on. He and his men raced across the Virginia fields being pursued by the Union Army. Hesitant to accept defeat, they hung on to the bitter end; however, they simply didn't have the means to continue the fight. The Confederacy had lost hope, and so General Lee had to surrender to Grant at Appomattox in Virginia.

Confederate soldiers being pursued by Union soldiers.

THE CONFEDERACY

43

FREEDOM FOR SLAVES

After 200 years of slavery, slaves in America were freed when the 13th amendment was added to the constitution. It stated that "Neither slavery nor involuntary servitude, except as a punishment for crime where of the party shall have been duly convicted, shall exist within the United States, or any place subject to their jurisdiction."

How did the slaves embrace freedom ?

The slaves embraced their freedom by celebrating and parading. They embraced the political, educational, religious, and societal arenas from which they had previously been shunned. Prior to the Civil War, slaves had been denied full membership in many churches. Afterwards, they founded their own churches. They were able to serve as ministers and community leaders. They also began to take an active part in the political process where they were now allowed to vote and even hold governmental offices.

What were their voting rights ?

The 14th and 15th amendments provided for the equal rights of the freed slaves. This included the right to vote. The following clause was included in the 15th Amendment, article 1 and stated: "The right... to vote shall not be denied or abridged... on account of race, color, or previous condition of servitude." (the "previous condition of servitude" meant that states could not deny the right to vote to people who had been slaves). The freed slaves voted in large numbers and were active in conventions.

Who threatened the free slaves ?

Most white people from the South swallowed their resentment against the newfound freedom of the slaves and their participation in government. However, the Ku Klux Klan was the most notorious and widespread of the Southern vigilante groups. Their goals were to destroy the Republican party, throw out the Reconstruction governments, assist the planter class, and totally prevent the freed slaves from exercising their political rights. This group killed approximately 20,000 men, women, and children to achieve their goals.

The Ku Klux Klan.

What was Reconstruction

The Reconstruction was the period of time in which the United States began to rebuild following the Civil War, and lasted from 1865 to 1877. The term also refers to the process the federal government utilized to readmit the Confederate states back to the Union. What complicated the Reconstruction process was the fact that Abraham Lincoln, Andrew Johnson, and the members of Congress all had differing ideas on how this process should be handled. Lincoln favored a lenient policy. However, Andrew Johnson, his successor, had devised his own plan, and believed that "white men alone must manage the South."

How did the nation reunite

After the congressional Reconstruction plan that included the drafting of the Fourteenth Amendment which prevented states from denying rights and privileges to any U.S. citizen, state constitutional conventions met, and Southern voters elected new Republican dominated governments. By 1870, all of the former Confederate states had completed this process. The nation was reunited, but the Reconstruction was not over, because the Republicans wanted to make many economic changes in the South. This effort was pursued until the end of the Reconstruction in 1877.

A reunited nation with equality for everyone followed the Civil War.

FACT BYTES

Southern whites attacked the new rights, claiming that freed slaves controlled the government. The Freedmen's Bureau was set up by Congress to persuade the Southern states to recognize racial equality. Their agents monitored local and state legal affairs.

FREEDOM FOR SLAVES

GLOSSARY

Abolitionist
People who wanted to do away with slavery and end it forever. They didn't believe in slavery due to moral and ethical beliefs.

Army
The largest organizational group of soldiers, made up of one or more corps. There were 16 Union armies and 23 Confederate armies.

Artillery
Large mounted firearms operated by crews such as cannons or mortars. These were commonly used during the Civil War.

Assassinate
To murder a public figure by surprise attack, usually for political reasons. John Wilkes Booth assassinated President Lincoln.

Blockade
The shutting off of a place usually by troops or ships to prevent entrance or exit. Union warships blocked the southern coast.

Bombard
Attack with artillery or bombers. To fire cannons on a certain area for an extended period of time.

Border states
The states of Maryland, Kentucky, and Missouri.

Although these states did not officially join the Confederacy, many of their citizens supported the South.

Breech-loading
Rifle-muskets that could be loaded in the middle between the barrel and the stock instead of from the end.

Caliber
This is the distance around the inside of a gun barrel measured in thousands of an inch.

Campaign
This is a series of activities carried out to bring a particular result, such as Clara Barton's campaign.

Canister
A projectile, shot from a cannon, filled with about 35 marble-sized iron balls that scattered like the pellets of a shotgun.

Cavalry
Troops moving on horseback. Mounted soldiers on horseback such as the cavalry soldiers in the Civil War.

Company
This is a group of 50 to 100 soldiers led by a captain. 10 companies = 1 regiment.

Confederacy
The Southern states that left the union of the United States to form the Confederate States of America.

Emancipation
This means to be set free, delivered, or discharged. The slaves longed for their emancipation.

Federal
This means loyal to the government of the United States. It also refers to the Union, Yankee, or Northern.

Garrison
This is a group of soldiers stationed at a military post.

Hardtack
This was a hard, typically worm-infested biscuit used by both Confederate and Union armies as a main source of food.

Haversack
This was a bag that was used by the soldiers to carry their food. Many soldiers carried this.

Industry
The making or manufacturing of goods. Much of this in done in factories such as were prominent in the North.

Infantry
This is a branch of the military in which soldiers travelled and fought on foot.

Ironclad
This is a ship or naval vessel protected by iron armor. These were used in the naval battles.

Militia
These are troops, like the National Guard, who are only called out to defend the land in an emergency.

Minie (ball) bullet
This was the standard infantry bullet of the Civil War. It was designed for muzzle-loading rifle-muskets.

Musket
This is a smoothbore firearm fired from the shoulder. Thrust from exploding powder shoots the bullet forward.

Muzzle-loading
These muskets had to be loaded from the end by putting the gunpowder and the bullet or ball down the barrel.

Navy
This is a branch of the military using ships to conduct warfare. During the Civil War, the battles on water were the Naval battles.

Officer
Ranking soldiers who were able to issue commands. They were the soldiers who oversaw and provided orders to the others.

Parole
This is a pledge by a prisoner of war or a defeated soldier not to bear arms weapons and fight.

Percussion
Percussion means striking. A gun that uses a hammer to strike a cap is a percussion arm.

Plantation
A large farm in the South. Most of the work done on a plantation was done by slaves.

Popular sovereignty
This term referred to the States having the right to choose whether to allow slavery. This term referred to states' rights.

Private
This is the lowest rank in the army. A private soldier is the soldier with the lowest rank.

Rebel
This was a person loyal to the Confederate States. Also known as a Southern or Confederate.

Reconstruction
The period from 1865-1877 when the Confederate states were rebuilt and reunited with the Union.

Regiment
This was the basic organizational unit of both Confederate and Union forces consisting of approximately 1,000 men.

Republican party
This was formed in the 1850s to fight against the extension of slavery. They also fought for higher tariffs. This party elected Lincoln in 1860.

Revolver
A handheld firearm with a chamber to hold multiple bullets. The chamber turns so that each bullet can be fired repeatedly in succession without reloading.

Rifled cannon
This type of cannon had a grooved barrel enabling one to shoot cannon balls highly accurately.

Secession
This term refers to leaving or seceding from the Union. The South seceded from the Union during the Civil War.

Shell
A hollow projectile, shot from a cannon. A shell was filled with powder and lit by a fuse when it was fired.

Siege
This term means to surround and cut off supplies to an army or town until they surrender.

Slavery
A state of bondage in which African Americans were owned by other people, and forced to work laboriously on their behalf.

Smooth bore
This is a type of musket or cannon with a smooth barrel, able to shoot round lead balls and highly inaccurate.

States rights
The belief that the powers of the individual states were greater than the powers of the Federal government.

Surrender
To admit defeat and give up in the face of overwhelming odds. Lee surrendered to Grant at the conclusion of the Civil War.

Territory
This was the land within the mainland boundaries of the country that had not yet become a state by 1861.

Union
This is the term that referred to the Northern states during the Civil War. The Union won the Civil War.

Volunteer
Someone who does something because they want to, not because they need to do it. Most Civil War soldiers were volunteers.

West Point
The United States Military Academy at West Point, New York. It was the military school for more than 1,000 officers in the Civil War.

Yankee
his was a Northerner or someone loyal to the Federal government of the United States. Also known as Union, Federal, or Northern.

GLOSSARY

INDEX

Acknowledgements

Key: Top - t; middle - m; bottom - b; left - l; right -r. LC - Library of Congress, Prints & Photographs Division.

Front cover: (bl) Topham Picturepoint ; (br) Nicolas Forder; (tl, tr) Tria Giovan/Corbis.
Back cover: (mr) Topham Picturepoint. (tr, bl) Tria Giovan/Corbis. (ml) LC [4a40928u]. Illustrations by Mike Bell.

2: (bl) Topham Picturepoint. 5: (tr) LC-B8171-3608 DLC; (mr) LC-B8171-0383 DLC.6: (tl) LC-B8171-1321 DLC.
7: (tl) Topham Picturepoint. 8: (ml) LC-B8171-3061 DLC. 9: (mr) Topham Picturepoint. 10: (tl) Topham Picturepoint.
11: (tr) LC-B8184-10698 DLC. 12: (bl) LC-B8171-7035 DLC. 13: (tr) LC-B8171-0627 DLC. 16: (tl) LC-DIG-cwpb-02647
DLC. 17: (br) Topham Picturepoint. 18: (bl) Bettmann/CORBIS. 19: (tr) Topham Picturepoint. 21: (bm) LC-B8171-7861 DLC.
22: (br) LC-B8172-1630 DLC. 23: (br) Bettmann/CORBIS. 25: (br) LC [4a40928u]. 27: (bl) LC-B8171-3283 DLC; (br) LC-
B8171-7681. 30: (tl) Bettmann/CORBIS; (bl) LC-B8171-2513 DLC. 32: (ml) O'Sullivan, Timothy H./LC-B8171-0762 DLC;
(br) LC-B8171-7822 DLC. 34: (tl) Topham Picturepoint. 36: (tl) Topham Picturepoint. 37: (mr) LC-B8171-2348 DLC]; (br) LC-
B8184-10455 DLC. 38: (bl) LC-B8184-7964-A DLC. 39: (bl) LC-B8172-0001 DLC; (br) LC-B8172-1467 DLC.
41: (bl) Topham Picturepoint. 42: (bl) LC-B8171-7292 DLC. 43: (tr) Topham Picturepoint. 44: (br) Topham Picturepoint.
45: (br) Topham Picturepoint. Illustrations by Mike Bell.